C000175371

Securing Mobile Banking Using Image Steganography

A Case Study of Alat by Wema Bank Mobile Application

LAP LAMBERT Academic Publishing

Cover image: www.ingimage.com

Publisher:
LAP LAMBERT Academic Publishing
is a trademark of
International Book Market Service Ltd., member of OmniScriptum Publishing Group
17 Meldrum Street, Beau Bassin 71504, Mauritius

Printed at: see last page
ISBN: 978-620-0-50500-2

SECURING MOBILE BANKING USING IMAGE STEGANOGRAPHY (A CASE STUDY OF ALAT BY WEMA MOBILE BANKING)

BY: AYOMIDE ADEFE

DEPARTMENT OF COMPUTER SCIENCE FEDERAL UNIVERSITY OF TECHNOLOGY AKURE.

SUPERVISOR: DR. R.O. AKINYEDE

OCTOBER, 2018

DEDICATION

This project work is dedicated to my Father, Rev. S.O. ADEFE who made it as a matter of necessity to pursue my bachelors' degree.

ACKNOWLEDGEMENT

I give sincere appreciation to God Almighty for his unending grace and sufficient blessings all through my project.

I sincerely give thanks to my supervisor Dr. R.O Akinyede for his patience in making meaningful inputs to this work; thanks for your assistance, supervision, guidance, words of advice, the corrections you made, and the time you devoted to this project work. I am also grateful to the Head of Department, Dr. S.A Oluwadare and to all lecturers and technologists in the Department of Computer Science, Federal University of Technology, Akure who made the project work a smooth one.

I appreciate my parents Reverend and Mrs. S.O Adefe for their prayers, moral and financial support. I also appreciate my sister and her husband for their moral and financial support.

Special thanks to Pastor A.A Ibosiola for his guidance, prayer and moral support, and also to all my friends and members of CACCF FUTA who in one way or the other contributed to the success of this work.

ABSTRACT

The internet has played a key role in changing how we do business today, as a result of the internet; there has been continuous growth in number of customers who use mobile banking due to it convenience. The challenge that opposes mobile banking is that private information's and data are sent directly to customers in plain text form. Developing a secure mobile banking system will help in reducing some of the problems associated with internet and bank frauds while making customers less concern and "worry-free" about the security of their funds and confidential information. The purpose of this research work is to develop a safe and secure mobile banking platform based on image steganography. The system is designed upon key players in the banking setting and it is implemented using Java, NetBeans, and Google firebase as it backend database. The encoding and decoding of the digital image was based on Least Significant Bit algorithm. The project was able to provide a secure mobile banking system for both the bank and their customers.

TABLE OF CONTENT

CHAPTER FIVE: CONCLUSION AND RECOMMENDATION

LIST OF FIGURES

LIST OF TABLES

CHAPTER ONE

INTRODUCTION

1.1   BACKGROUND OF THE STUDY

The banking industry is on the edge of another fintech revolution (Mohammed & Ganesh, 2011). Mobile banking is already going mainstream, and while the idea of mobile banking may not seem as exciting as say, sending a person to the moon, it is still a major shift that is already having a big impact on the banking industry. Mobile banking provides a more secure platform than the traditional ATMs (Felix and Irwin, 2015). With the growing prevalence of "skimmers" — devices that can intercept personal details while running your card through an ATM — a mobile banking system defeats such scams (Felix and Irwin, 2015).

A number of major financial institutions are continuing to innovate with mobile banking card less ATM capabilities, allowing customers to withdraw money from an ATM using a mobile app to initiate the transaction (Neenu, 2014). Commercial banks in Nigeria are taking a number of approaches to card less ATMs transactions with the aid of mobile banking, including enabling customers to log in to their banking app with their username and password to request a one-time passcode that the customer inputs into the ATM to complete their transaction (Felix and Irwin, 2015), one of such bank is **Wema**. In the first quarter of year 2017 Wema bank launched "Alat" a digital bank powered by them. Alat has many features, but one of it prominent feature is the ability to perform card less transactions.

Wema bank saw card less ATMs which is one of the features of mobile banking as a way to improve the customer experience by eliminating the need to carry and replace cards, which can be easily lost or compromised, as well as reduce the cost to the institution to replace them. They also look at this as a means to leverage opportunities for increased engagement at the customer's preferred channel (Phillip, 2017).

A lot of the new technology surrounding the mobile banking card less transactions is aimed at reducing the threat of fraud while improving consumers' security and convenience (Krishnaveni and Sathyadevi, 2017). Of course, anything that can make the process more streamlined and more cost-effective for the banks is good, too, considering their operating costs have an impact

1

on their customers. But just like the traditional ATMs, this new card less transaction on mobile banking that was recently piloted by Alat has already come under attack from identity thieves who have successfully stolen customers' money.

Theft of ATMs and use of credit card skimmers made the traditional ATMs very prone to fraud but like I said earlier, card less transaction has also been compromised by identity thieves who use it to commit fraud (Satish, 2012).

The fraud works like this; by gaining access to the Alat mobile banking username and password, thieves open the bank's app on their phones. They add their own mobile phone number to the user account, after this they generate a pay code and a pin which the bank send to their mobile phone number, and then conduct the transaction at an ATM from anywhere they choose. It's hard to prove one's innocence when one's account is drained because "you" added the phone number and "you" made the withdrawal at an ATM.

Several security tactics develop to help combat fraud targeting card less ATM transactions at the point of access (the mobile device) include; **biometrics**, **Permanent device ID** (a way to identify a device using its unique attributes in order to establish the first layer of trust by fulfilling the "something you have" factor in a multifactor solution), **Customer Behaviour Analysis** (Krishnaveni and Sathyadevi, 2017).

Image Steganography, as a means of securing mobile banking card less transaction was born out of Information Security research as other tactics listed above were vulnerable to hacks, expensive(biometrics) and generally not reliable (Saranya and Thirumal, 2014). Steganography is the art of hiding secret or sensitive information into digital media like images so as to have secure communication (Nagham, et al, 2012). In steganography we hide our secret information in some cover image such that one cannot track the message. The original Image is called cover image and the image in which message is embedded is called Stego Image (Kaur & Kumar, 2016). Steganography can also be done with Text, video, audio and protocol steganography.
In order to protect customers, the pay code and the pin been generated on the Alat mobile banking which will be sent to the registered mobile phone number is encrypted and sent in a digital media preferably an image.

2

1.2 MOTIVATION

Neenu and Harsh (2014). Card less Cash Access Using Biometric ATM Security System.

The objective of this research work is to design a biometric ATM system which enables cash withdrawal at an ATM without using existing magnetic swipe cards, to provide an alternative approach to access cash via OTP generation on user's phone in case of loss of pin. The scheme made use of two techniques, namely Cryptography and Steganography. AES 256 encryption algorithm is the main encryption used. It also made use of Neural Networks for Fingerprint recognition. This paper concludes that the conventional ATM system needs to be replaced with Biometric systems where the transaction process becomes easier, reliable, secure, and eliminating the need of carrying any kind of swipe cards. However, biometrics features are not perfect for verification on ATM, and the research does not include authentication.

Innocent and Adewale. (2016). Securing Card less Automated Teller Machine Transactions Using Bimodal Authentication System.

The objective of this research work is to reduce the huge and recurrent card possession and repossession cost incurred by Bank Customers. It used inference mechanism for the reasoning process. At the end of this research, a more secured and cost effective card less transaction was proposed at the end of this project work. However, the lack of universality of some characteristics (for instance, in the case of fingerprints, approximately 4% of people cannot enlist because of weak fingerprints, and this per cent increases at 7% in the case of the iris).

Prerana and Nikumbh. (2015). Security System in ATM using Multimodal Biometric System and Steganographic Technique.

The objective of this research work is to provide protection to the biometric template and to enhance the security in the ATM system with Multi-biometrics. Person Authentication System based on multimodal biometric and steganography, it involve; Data Protection system using bits wraps algorithm, Iris with palm print recognition based on wavelet packet and Weber's local descriptor. At the end of this research work, a multimodal security system for recognition and authentication purpose using iris and palm print biometric traits by Wavelet Transform and Weber's Local Descriptor, in ATM system was designed; this system provides better data protection and less complexity. However, Cost of installing Multimodal Security system is high.

3

Noisy signals captured from the sensors due to the incorrect usage by the clients and due to the environmental conditions (humidity, dirt, dust etc.); the lack of the safety of the used sensors.

Furthermore, we live in a rapidly changing country that is gradually becoming a global hub and mobile banking and card less transaction is now a household name and a must for everybody in order to achieve the propose cashless policy.

The online banking industry has grown rapidly over the past years, and will continue to experience increase as financial institutions continue to encourage customers to do online banking transactions such as money transfer, access information about the account or otherwise as well as payment of monthly bills.

Sadly Internet criminals and fraudsters are using this new trend in technology to steal customer's personal information and commit fraud. Hence, there is need to enhance security and customer trust in mobile banking (card less transaction).

1.3   OBJECTIVES OF THE STUDY

The objectives for this research work are to:

i.   design a system plain and sensitive information (pay-code and pin) of a mobile banking card less transaction will be secured.

ii.   implement the above design in (I) by using LSB for encoding and decoding, netbeans IDE for coding of my java programming language.

1.4   METHODOLOGY

A detailed literature review on the history and emergence of steganography, types of steganography, application of steganography, mobile banking, benefits of mobile banking, channels through which mobile banking services are deployed, risks associated with mobile banking, types of security frameworks available and widely applied on mobile banking application was carried out from journals, articles and related materials. The data collected in view of the research objectives was used to develop a portal where images are steganographed and de-steganographed in order to resist unauthorized access and modification of sensitive customers' information and to prevent identity theft.

The design stage involves the review of the architecture platform for the implementation and design of the de-steganography platform. Least significant bit which is the process of adjusting the least significant bit pixels of the cover image is the Image steganography technique that will be used. It is a simple technique for embedding message into an image.

Implementation stage is the continuation of the design stage but under which the main activity is being carried on and involves the gathering of all the necessary information's.

The tools used include:

   i.   Netbeans IDE,

  ii.   Java programming language,

 iii.   Firebase cloud database system.

 iv.   Android Studio

Testing will be carried out after the implementation of the design.

1.5 Contribution to Knowledge

At the end of the research, the following contribution would have been made to knowledge:

a. Provide better and a more secure means of sending sensitive information from bank to customers' via the internet.

b. Proposal of a better security frame work using image steganography, that will benefit banks to offer more secured mobile banking services to customers, increase the number of customers using the mobile banking technologies and protects customers from hackers and third party access to their account information.

CHAPTER TWO

LITERATURE OVERVIEW

2.1 GENERAL OVERVIEW OF STEGANOGRAPHY.

Since the ".com" boom in the early 90's which has caused a steady rise in the use of internet and development of technology at a fast pace, security of information has been the utmost priority (Morkel, 2005). The data needs to be kept secure and safe so that it could be accessed only by the authorized personnel and any unauthorized user cannot have any access of that data (Nagham, et al, 2012). Data sharing is increasing as thousands of messages and data is being transmitted on internet every day from one place to another. The protection of data is prime concern of the sender (Kaur, 2016). The need is that correct data should be sent but in a secret way that only the receiver should be able to understand the message (Kaur, 2016). This urgent need to secure information brought about cryptography, which was created as a technique for securing the secrecy of communication and many different methods have been developed to encrypt and decrypt data in order to keep the message secret (Shazmeen, 2012). Although, this method has been effective overtime it is sometimes not enough to keep the contents of a message secret. There is a necessity to keep the existence of the message completely secret and unknown to an unauthorized receiver. The technique used to implement this is called **steganography**.

Steganography is the art and science of invisible communication (Doshi, et al, 2012). This is accomplished through hiding information in other information, thus hiding the existence of the communicated information. The word steganography is derived from the Greek words "stegos" meaning "cover" and "grafia" meaning "writing" defining it as "covered writing.

According to (Kaur, et al, 2016), the method of hiding information has a long history. The Greek historian Herodotus wrote of a nobleman named Histaeus, who needed to communicate with his son-in-law in Greece. He shaved the head of one of his most trusted slaves and tattooed the message onto his scalp. When the slave's hair grew back the slave was dispatched with the hidden message. In the Second World War the Microdot technique was developed by the Germans. Information, especially photographs, was reduced in size until it was the size of a typed period. Extremely difficult to detect, a normal cover message was sent over an insecure channel with one of the periods on the paper containing hidden information. Today

6

steganography is mostly used on computers with digital data being the carriers and networks being the high speed delivery channels.

Steganography differs from cryptography in the sense that where cryptography focuses on keeping the contents of a message secret, steganography focuses on keeping the existence of a message secret (Moorthy, et al, 2013). Cryptography and steganography are both method to protect information from unwanted parties. Once the presence of hidden information is noticed or even suspected, the purpose of steganography is has been defeated (Kaur, 2016). Two other technologies that are closely related to steganography are watermarking and fingerprinting (Maganbhai, 2015). These technologies are mainly concerned with the protection of intellectual property, thus the algorithms have different requirements than steganography.

In watermarking all of the instances of an object are "marked" in the same way. The kind of information hidden in objects when using watermarking is usually a signature to signify origin or ownership for the purpose of copyright protection. While in fingerprinting, different unique marks are embedded in distinct copies of the carrier object that are supplied to different customers, this enables the intellectual property owner to identify customers who break their licensing agreement by supplying the property to third parties.

In watermarking and fingerprinting the fact that information is hidden inside the files may be public knowledge sometimes it may even be visible while in steganography, the imperceptibility of the information is crucial (Morkel, 2005).

A successful attack on a steganographic system consists of an adversary observing that there is information hidden inside a file, while a successful attack on a watermarking or fingerprinting system would not be to detect the mark, but to remove it.

Lack of strength and constant breach in cryptography has driven the rise of more research in steganography.

2.2 APPLICATIONS OF STEGANOGRAPHY

According to (Kaur, et al, 2016) steganography is applied in fields listed below for the purpose of security and confidentiality:

i.   **Copyright Protection**: Copy protection mechanisms that prevent data, generally digital data, from being copied. Most of the newer applications use steganography like a watermark, to protect a copyright on information. Photo collections, sold on CD, often have hidden messages in the photos which allow detection of unauthorized use. The same technique applied to DVDs is even more effective, since the industry builds DVD recorders to detect and disallow copying of protected DVDs.

ii. **Feature Tagging**: Elements can be embedded inside an image, as the names of individuals in a photo or Locations in a map. Copy the stego-image also copies all of the embedded features and only parties who possess the decoding stego-key will be able to extract and view the features.

iii. **Secret Communication**: the use steganography does not advertise secret communication and therefore avoids scrutiny of the sender side, message, and recipient. A secret, blueprint, or other sensitive information can be transmitted without alerting potential attackers.

iv. **Use by terrorists**: Terrorists can also use steganography to keep their communications secret and to coordinate attacks. All of this sounds fairly nefarious, and in fact the obvious uses of steganography are for things like espionage

2.3 TYPES OF STEGANOGRAPHY

2.3.1 TEXT STEGANOGRAPHY

Text steganography is broadly classified into 3 basic categories

i.   Format-based
ii. Random and Statistical generation
iii. Linguistic Method.

1. Format-Based Method:

It uses the physical text formatting of text as a place in which to hide information. This method modifies existing text in order to hide the steganographic text. Insertion of spaces, deliberate misspellings distributed throughout the text, resizing the fonts are some of many format-based methods being used in text steganography. However, format-based methods can trick most human eyes but it can't once the computer systems have been used.

2. Random and Statistical Generation:

This is the process of generating cover text according to the statistical properties. This method is based on character sequence and word sequences. The hiding of information within character sequences is embedding the information to be appeared in random sequence of characters. This sequence must appear to be random to anyone who intercepts the message. A second approach for character generation is to take the statistical properties of word-length and letter frequency in order to create "words" (without lexical value) which will appear to have the same statistical properties as actual words in a given language. The hiding of information within word sequences, the actual dictionary items can be used to encode one or more bits of information per word using a codebook of mappings between lexical items and bit sequences, or words themselves can encode the hidden information.

3. Linguistic Method:

This method specifically considers the linguistic properties of generated and modified text, frequently uses linguistic structure as a place for hidden messages. steganographic data can be hidden within the syntactic structure itself. Example: Sender sends a series of integer number (Key) to the recipient with a prior agreement that the secret message is hidden within the respective position of subsequent words of the cover text. For example the series is „1, 1, 2, 3, 4, 2, 4"and the cover text is "A team of five men joined today". So the hidden message is "Atfvoa". A "0" in the number series will indicate a blank space in the recovered message. The word in the received cover text will be skipped if the number of characters in that word is less than the respective number in the series (Key) which shall also be skipped during the process of message unhide.

2.3.2 AUDIO STEGANOGRAPHY

Steganography, in general, relies on the imperfection of the human auditory and visual systems (Doshi, et al, 2012). Audio steganography takes advantage of the psychoacoustical masking

9

phenomenon of the human auditory system [HAS]. Psychoacoustical or auditory masking property renders a weak tone imperceptible in the presence of a strong tone in its temporal or spectral neighbourhood (Doshi, et al, 2012). This property arises because of the low differential range of the HAS even though the dynamic range covers 80 dB below ambient level. Frequency masking occurs when human ear cannot perceive frequencies at lower power level if these frequencies are present in the vicinity of tone- or noise-like frequencies at higher level. Additionally, a weak pure tone is masked by wide-band noise if the tone occurs within a critical band. This property of inaudibility of weaker sounds is used in different ways for embedding information. Embedding of data by inserting inaudible tones in cover audio signal has been presented recently. In audio steganography, secret message is embedded into digitized audio signal which result slight altering of binary sequence of the corresponding audio file. The list of methods that are commonly used for audio steganography are listed and discussed below.

i.   LSB coding
ii.   Parity coding
iii.   Phase coding
iv.   Spread spectrum
v.   Echo hiding

i.   LSB CODING

Sampling technique followed by Quantization converts analog audio signal to digital binary sequence.

ii.   PARITY CODING

Instead of breaking a signal down into individual samples, the parity coding method breaks a signal down into separate regions of samples and encodes each bit from the secret message in a sample region's parity bit. If the parity bit of a selected region does not match the secret bit to be encoded, the process flips the LSB of one of the samples in the region. Thus, the sender has more of a choice in encoding the secret bit, and the signal can be changed in a more unobtrusive fashion.

iii.   PHASE CODING

Human Auditory System (HAS) can't recognize the phase change in audio signal as easy it can recognize noise in the signal. The phase coding method exploits this fact. This technique encodes the secret message bits as phase shifts in the phase spectrum of a digital signal, achieving an inaudible encoding in terms of signal-to- noise ratio.

iv.   SPREAD SPECTRUM

In the context of audio steganography, the basic spread spectrum (SS) method attempts to spread secret information across the audio signal's frequency spectrum as much as possible. This is analogous to a system using an implementation of the LSB coding that randomly spreads the message bits over the entire sound file. However, unlike LSB coding, the SS method spreads the secret message over the sound file's frequency spectrum, using a code that is independent of the actual signal. As a result, the final signal occupies a bandwidth in excess of what is actually required for transmission.

v.   ECHO HIDING

In echo hiding, information is embedded in a sound file by introducing an echo into the discrete signal. Like the spread spectrum method, it too provides advantages in that it allows for a high data transmission rate and provides superior robustness when compared to the noise inducing methods. If only one echo was produced from the original signal, only one bit of information could be encoded. Therefore, the original signal is broken down into blocks before the encoding process begins. Once the encoding process is completed, the blocks are concatenated back together to create the final signal.

2.3.3 VIDEO STEGANOGRAPHY

Video files are generally a collection of images and sounds, so most of the presented techniques on images and audio can be applied to video files too. When information is hidden inside video the program or person hiding the information will usually use the DCT (Discrete Cosine Transform) method. DCT works by slightly changing each of the images in the video, only so

11

much that it is not noticeable by the human eye. To be more precise about how DCT works, DCT alters values of certain parts of the images, it usually rounds them up. For example, if part of an image has a value of 6.667 it will round it up to 7. The great advantages of video are the large amount of data that can be hidden inside and the fact that it is a moving stream of images and sounds. Therefore, any small but otherwise noticeable distortions might go by unobserved by humans because of the continuous flow of information.

2.3.4 IMAGE STAEGANOGRAPHY

The most widely used technique today is hiding of secret messages into a digital image. This steganography technique exploits the weakness of the human visual system (HVS). HVS cannot detect the variation in luminance of color vectors at collection of color pixels. The individual pixels can be represented by their optical higher frequency side of the visual spectrum. A picture can be represented by a characteristics like 'brightness', 'chroma' etc. Each of these characteristics can be digitally expressed in terms of 1s and 0s. For example: a 24-bit bitmap will have 8 bits, representing each of the three color values (red, green, and blue) at each pixel. If we consider just the blue there will be 2 different values of blue. The difference between 11111111 and 11111110 in the value for blue intensity is likely to be undetectable by the human eye. Hence, if the terminal recipient of the data is nothing but human visual system (HVS) then the Least Significant Bit (LSB) can be used for something else other than color information.

2.4 IMAGE STEGANOGRAPHY TECHNIQUES

Images are the most common cover objects used for steganography. In the domain of digital images, many different image file format exist. Most of them for specific applications, different image file formats have different steganographic algorithms.

2.4.1 Spatial Domain Methods:

There are many versions of spatial steganography, all directly change some bits in the image pixel values in hiding data. Least significant bit (LSB) - based steganography is one of the simplest techniques that hides a secret message in the LSBs of pixel values without introducing many perceptible distortions. Changes in the value of the LSB are imperceptible for human eyes. Spatial domain techniques are broadly classified into:

i. Least Significant Bit (LSB)

ii. Pixel value differencing (PVD)

iii. Edges based data embedding method

iv. Random pixel embedding method

v. Mapping pixel to hidden data method

vi. Labelling or connectivity method

vii. Pixel intensity based method

viii. Texture based method

ix. Histogram shifting methods

2.4.1.1 LEAST SIGNIFICANT BIT (LSB):

Least significance bit (LSB)-based steganography is one of the simplest techniques that hide a secret message in the LSBs of pixel values by introducing imperceptible distortions. The major drawback of this technique is the amount of additive noise that creeps in the cover image, having direct impact on the PSNR and the statistical properties of the image. These embedding techniques often can be easily destroyed by compression, filtering or a less than perfect format or size conversion. The least significant bit (in other words, the 8th bit) of some or all of the bytes inside an image is changed to a bit of the secret message. When using a 24-bit image, a bit of each of the red, green and blue colour components can be used, since they are each represented by a byte. In other words, one can store 3 bits in each pixel. An 800 × 600 pixel image, can thus store a total amount of 1,440,000 bits or 180,000 bytes of embedded data.

A very good example to Consider is a 3- pixel grid in a 24- bit image:

00110011 01100011 01101111

01101110 01101100 00110100

01101101 01100101 01101011

Suppose we want to hide a character 'y' in the image. The ASCII code of 'y' is 121 whose binary value is 01111001.Now pixels after embedding the message in the image are as shown below:

00110010 01100011 01101111
01101111 01101101 00110100
01101100 01100101 01101011

8 bits were to be embedded in the image however only 4 bits were changed. Thus on an average only half of the bits are changed in the embedding process.

Considering another example of a grid for 3 pixels of a 24-bit image:

(00101101 00011100 11011100)

(10100110 11000100 00001100)

(11010010 10101101 01100011)

When the number 200, which binary representation is 11001000, is embedded into the least significant bits of this part of the image, the resulting grid is as follows:

(00101101 00011101 11011100)

(10100110 11000101 00001100)

(11010010 10101100 01100011)

Although the number was embedded into the first 8 bytes of the grid, only the 3 underlined bits needed to be changed according to the embedded message. On average, only half of the bits in an image will need to be modified to hide a secret message using the maximum cover size.

The two approaches above are very easy to detect. A slightly more secure system is for the sender and the receiver to share a secret key that specifies only certain pixels to be changed. Should an attacker suspect that LSB steganography has been used, he has no way of knowing which pixels to target without knowing the secret key.

In its simplest form, LSB makes use of BMP images, since they use lossless compression. Unfortunately to be able to hide a secret message inside a BMP file, one would require a very large cover image. Nowadays, BMP images of 800 × 600 pixels are not often used on the Internet and might arouse suspicion. For this reason, LSB steganography has also been developed for use with other image file formats.

Pros of using LSB:

    a. It is robust in nature.

    b. It can hide large amount of data.

c. There is less chance for degradation of the original image.

Cons of using LSB:

    a. Hidden data can be easily destroyed by simple attacks.

    b. Changes in image can lose data.

According to (Morkel, et al, 2005), there are some requirements which we use to define the imperceptibility of an algorithm. These requirements are as follows:

i.   Invisibility: The strength of steganography lies in its ability to be unnoticed by human eye. The moment that one can see that an image has been tampered with, the algorithm has been compromised. Invisibility of a steganographic algorithm is the foremost requirement.

ii.   Payload capacity: unlike watermarking, steganography aims at hidden communication and therefore requires sufficient embedding capacity.

iii.   Robustness against statistical attacks: Statistical steganalysis is the practice of detecting hidden information through applying statistical tests on image data. Many steganographic algorithms leave a signature when embedding information that can be easily detected through statistical analysis.

iv.   Robustness against image manipulation: Image manipulation, such as cropping or rotating can be performed on the image before it reaches its destination. These manipulations may destroy the hidden message. Steganographic algorithm has to be robust against either malicious or unintentional changes to the image.

v.   Independent of file format: Suspicion might arise if only one type of file format is continuously communicated between two parties. A good and reliable steganographic algorithm must have the ability to embed information in any type of file.

vi.   Unsuspicious files: This requirement includes all characteristics of a steganographic algorithm that may result in images that are not used normally and may cause suspicion.

Table 2.1: comparison of image steganography algorithms

	LSB in BMP	LSB in GIF	JPEG compression	Patchwork	Spread spectrum

Invisibility	High*	Medium*	High	High	High
Payload capacity	High	Medium	Medium	Low	Medium
Robustness against statistical attacks	Low	Low	Medium	High	High
Robustness against image manipulations	Low	Low	Medium	High	Medium
Independent of file format	Low	Low	Low	High	High
Unsuspicious files	Low	Low	High	High	High

*- Depends on cover image used

The levels at which the algorithms satisfy the requirements are defined as high, medium and low. A high level means that the algorithm completely satisfies the requirement, while a low level indicates that the algorithm has a weakness in this requirement. A medium level indicates that the requirement depends on outside influences, for example the cover image used. LSB in GIF images has the potential of hiding a large message, but only when the most suitable cover image has been chosen.

Table 2.2: Showing application of LSB in different file formats

	Suggested applications
LSB in BMP	LSB in BMP is most suitable for applications where the focus is on the amount of information to be transmitted and not on the secrecy of that information.
LSB in GIF	LSB in GIF is a very efficient algorithm to use

	when embedding a reasonable amount of data in a greyscale image.
JPEG compression	The JPEG file format can be used for most applications of steganography, but is especially suitable for images that have to be communicated over an open systems environment like the internet.
Patchwork	Patchwork is most suitable for transmitting a small amount of very sensitive information.
Spread spectrum	Spread spectrum techniques can be used for most steganography applications, although its highly mathematical and intricate approach may prove too much for some.

Source: Advance LSB Knowledge

2.4.2 Transfer Domain Technique:

This is a more complex way of hiding information in an image (Gandharba, et al, 2014). Various algorithms and transformations are used on the image to hide information in it. Transform domain embedding can be termed as a domain of embedding techniques for which a number of algorithms have been suggested. The process of embedding data in the frequency domain of a signal is much stronger than embedding principles that operate in the time domain. It is worth saying that most of the strong steganographic systems today operate within the transform domain. Transform domain techniques have an advantage over LSB techniques because they hide information in areas of the image that are less exposed to compression, cropping, and image processing. Some transform domain techniques do not seem dependent on the image format and they may outrun lossless and lossy format conversions. The JPEG file format is the most common image file format on the internet owing to the small size of resultant images obtained by using it.

Transform domain techniques are broadly classified into:
  i.   Discrete Fourier transformation technique (DFT).
  ii. Discrete cosine transformation technique (DCT).

17

iii.   Discrete Wavelet transformation technique (DWT).

iv.   Lossless or reversible method (DCT).

v.   Embedding in coefficient bits.

2.4.3 Distortion Technique:

Distortion techniques need knowledge of the original cover image during the decoding process where the decoder functions to check for differences between the original cover image and the distorted cover image in order to restore the secret message. The encoder adds a sequence of changes to the cover image. So, information is described as being stored by signal distortion. Using this technique, a stego object is created by applying a sequence of modifications to the cover image. This sequence of modifications is use to match the secret message required to transmit. The message is encoded at pseudo-randomly chosen pixels. If the stego-image is different from the cover image at the given message pixel, the message bit is a "1." otherwise, the message bit is a "0." The encoder can modify the "1" value pixels in such a manner that the statistical properties of the image are not affected. However, the need for sending the cover image limits the benefits of this technique. In any steganographic technique, the cover image should never be used more than once. If an attacker tampers with the stego-image by cropping, scaling or rotating, the receiver can easily detect it. In some cases, if the message is encoded with error correcting information, the change can even be reversed and the original message can be recovered.

2.4.4 Masking and Filtering:

These techniques hide information by marking an image, in the same way as to paper watermarks. These techniques embed the information in the more significant areas than just hiding it into the noise level. The hidden message is more integral to the cover image. Watermarking techniques can be applied without the fear of image destruction due to lossy compression as they are more integrated into the image.

2.5   Mobile Banking:

Financial services and transactions through mobile device are called Mobile banking.

Mobile banking can be broken into three key areas namely: Informational, Transactional and Service, Marketing and Acquisition (Wendy, 2005). Within the area of informational there are functions such as balance and transaction history, loan, mortgage, and credit information, ATM and branch locators, as well as personal financial management (PFM) functions such as spending comparisons with peers or budget tools. Transactional services included account transfers, bill pay, person to person payments and remote deposit capture. Service features included functions that enhance the customer's experience including contact options, help information, and alerts. Additional service features include product renewal notifications, balance triggered savings offers, balance triggered credit offers, and location triggered travel insurance options. Finally, relative to marketing and acquisition, there are services such as mobile coupons/incentives, barcodes, new product information, customer research, cross selling and acquisition. The aspects of mobile that make it particularly appealing to marketing are the very personal nature of mobile devices and the "always on" aspect of customer use.

Mobile banking and Internet banking are very similar, except you are using a smart phone to bank alternately the computer. The applications of many smartphones connect you directly to your bank and allow you to transfer money. In the mobile banking option we can be transacting our amount anytime, anybody and anywhere.

2.5.1 Benefits of mobile banking:

i. Saving time and saving energy.
ii. Easy to use.
iii. Reduce cost.
iv. More suitable than internet-banking.

2.5.2 Channels through which mobile banking services are deployed:

i. Credit/Debit Alerts. □
ii. Minimum Balance Alerts. □
iii. Bill Payment Alerts.
iv. Bill Payment. □
v. Recent Transaction History Requests.

19

vi.   Information Requests like Interest Rates/Exchange Rates.

vii.   Account Balance Enquiry □□

viii.   Fund Transfer between Accounts.

2.6   Risks associated with Mobile Banking:

A. Malware

Malware is the term for maliciously crafted software code. Moreover, it is possible to perform the following operations for this type of malicious software Account information theft.

    i.   Fake web site substitution

    ii.   Account hijacking

B. TCP/IP Spoofing

An attacker gains unauthorized access to a mobile device or a network by making it show up that a malicious message has come from a trusted machine by spoofing the IP address of that machine.

C. Backdoors

Access to mobile program that avoided security mechanisms is a backdoor. A programmer may sometimes install a back door so that the program can be accessed for troubleshooting or other purposes. Back doors have been used by attackers to install themselves, as chunk of an exploit.

D. Tampering

It is an international modification of products in a way that would make them harmful to the consumer.

E. Social Engineering and Trojans

Trojans act as an authorized program, can delete, block, modify and copy data.

F. Malicious Applications

G. Privacy violations relative to application collection and distribution of data

H. SMS vulnerabilities

I. Payments infrastructure/ecosystem

2.7 Current Security Frameworks Applied on Mobile Banking Application are:

A. User name and PIN Security

It is something the user knows is often associated with any characters like a name, number. PINs should never be stored or processed in the clear anywhere in a system. Hash values of PINs should be encrypted to guard against brute-force attacks. Through PIN user is authenticated to the mobile network and he/she is protected from lost and theft. There are numerous of attacks that can jeopardize user confidentiality and security. Some of the attacks are brute force attacks where attackers try to log into the service with every possible password until he/she succeed. Additionally, more threats can emerge if original password that is provided by use during registration is stored in an inappropriate manner. One major problem with password and security is user factor. In most cases user is required to choose password that he/she will use on the system and remember it. PIN that is chosen can greatly influence security of the user, and because of that it is very important for user to choose strong password.

B. One Time Password (OTP)

OTP is a Random 6 digit number that changes every time, whenever user logs on the system and new password is generated and sent to the user on his mobile phone. OTP are utilized as an additional factor in multi-factor authorization/authentication applications. They are only valid for exactly one authorization or authentication request. The method of generating OTP whenever the user initiates a M-Banking transaction: - first step is the user enters his/her user name and password and allowed to login onto his webpage of his personal account, if the user authentication is valid. The user then initiates a transaction and the bank server responds back with OTP to his/her mobile phone. This is the second level of authentication done to avoid password thefts. The user then authenticates with the OTP himself. The OTP is checked at the server and the transaction proceeds if valid. The OTP id valid only time every next time user logs in he needs to provide a new OTP that the user would have received at that particular moment of time. Threats to OTP are: wireless interception- the GSM technology is insecure due to several vulnerabilities such as a lack of mutual authentication and weave encryption algorithms. Mobile phone Trojans- malware and especially Trojans that are designed to intercept SMS messages contains OTPs.

C. Biometric Authentication

Biometrics is the science and technology of measuring and analyzing human body characteristics such as fingerprints, retina venial patterns, irises, voice patterns, facial patterns, and hand/finger measurements for authentication or identification purpose. Biometric identify people by measuring some aspect of individual anatomy or physiology (hand geometry of finger, voice, face). A biometric system is essentially a pattern recognition system that operates by acquiring biometric data from an individual, extracting a feature set from the acquiring data, and comparing this feature set against the template set in the database. The main benefits of Biometrics technology are to provide a better security and to facilitate the authentication process for a user. It is usually difficult to copy the biometric characteristics of an individual than most of other authentication methods such as passwords.

2.8 ALAT by WEMA Mobile Banking Application:

ALAT is Nigeria's first fully functional digital bank. With ALAT, you can do all your banking transactions without being physically present at a bank. ALAT is built from scratch to be entirely digital, making all banking services available to you anywhere you can access the internet. In comparison, a banking app only offers some banking services (typically airtime purchases, bill payments and transfers). With a banking app, you usually still need to go to a physical bank to get a debit card and activate it, submit documents and often, to get some kinds of customer support but with ALAT customers don't need to go through such stress. Debit card can be activated online and delivered anywhere anytime. It supports Ios and android devices.

2.9 RELATED WORKS

Omariba, Masese and Wanyebi, (2012) Security and Privacy of Electronic Banking.

The objective of this research is to provide an effective and secure banking transaction by resolving four key technology issues which are; Security, Anonymity (Privacy), Authentication and Divisibility. The research was motivated by Need to provide effective and secure banking transactions, e-services provider's lack of security control which allows damaging privacy losses, frequent Misuse of consumers' confidential information, as in identity theft. At the end of this research, an electronic banking platform where users are able to interact with their banks "worry-free" and banks are operated under one common standard was proposed. However, the platform didn't provide enough security for consumers; consumers have to be more vigilant when doing business online. Also if the development team are not proactive and reactive in handling security threats, there might be attacks on the platform.

Shazmeen and shyam, (2012) A Practical Approach for Secure Internet Banking based on Cryptography.

The objective of the research work is to design a challenge/response-based short time password authentication methods using Symmetric cryptography in combination with Software security model. The research work was motivated by Online banking applications sending data directly to customers in plain text, Social engineering attack on electronic banking. At the end of the research need for security testing for online banking was emphasized, a new internet banking system which provides better authentication and identification was developed which allows user to carry out all banking transaction securely from anywhere, anytime in spite of the growing number of attacks and consequent frauds. However, the system make use of customer application supported handset for decryption, if the handset get stolen the system might be compromised. Also, the system doesn't provide much security for the bank user as most of the attacks directed at online banking systems target the user which is the weakest link.

Billa, (2012) Security Issues in Mobile Banking.

The objective of the work to identify security risk in Mobile Banking and to provide an authentication method for mobile banking transaction by using biometric mechanism. The major contribution of the proposed biometric mechanism is a finger-print scanning device which can identify the customer's finger print thus enabling the customer to access mobile banking services. However, the limitation of the work is that, it is applied only on those mobile devices which have finger print scanner.

Sarhan, Ahmed and Safwant, (2015) Secured Android Based Mobile Banking Scheme.

The objective of this research work is to provide security services including; confidentiality, integrity, and authentication between the financial institutions' servers and the mobile device used by the customer. Customers' communication mostly is through unsecured networks such as the Internet, Vulnerability of mobile phones to cyber-crimes, Users' confidential information has been at risk due to fixed values-based security schemes, one level authentication, separate hard token-based authentication, hardware stealing, and Android-Based attacks motivated the research work. At the end of the research solutions to mitigate most of the risks in the motivations were provided. It also specifies a comprehensive sought of how mobile banking schemes can be assessed. However, using RSA in mobile applications overloads the mobile set as it has a very long key 1024 bits to achieve a suitable level of security for M-Banking.

Krishnaveni and Sathyadevi, (2017) Mobile Banking and its Security

The objective of this research work is to develop tough security procedures to defend and protect customers' account, develop a cost-effective and application option for banking process with the aid of QR code. The research work was motivated by Security shortfalls in the present mobile banking implementations. At the end of this research, difference between using smartphone as a platform for authentication, using near field communication (NFC) and other applications in banking processes as well as security of each were made known. However, Software updates automatically and it may get compromised during this process.

Bhosale, (2012) Security in E-Banking via Card less Biometric ATMs

The objectives of this study are; to study scope of biometric authentication techniques in ATMs, to generate module which helps for simple operation of ATMs with full proof secure authentication via networking, providing suggestions with advantages and limitations of proposed model. The work was motivated due to need for new innovative model for biometric ATMs which can replace card system by biometric technology for operating ATMs. At the end of this research, a card less e-banking technique for ATMs was proposed which reduces efforts of handling, operating and various risks associated with cards. The same and simplified procedure will be helpful for Internet, Mobile and POS transactions. Due to unique method of authentication it reduces cost, time, and efforts of both banks as well as service users. However, this method is costlier and requires more instruments to be installed in ATM centres. Also due to biometric only account holder (except nominee) can access account.

Rao, GurleenKour and DivyaJyoti, (2011) One Time Password Security through Cryptography for Mobile Banking

The objective of the work is to build a software application model for performing high security mobile banking services. The major contribution of the work is the concept of One Time Password, which is every time a new password is generated and sent to the user on his mobile phone. The OTP is a random of 6 digits number that changes every time, whenever user logs on to the system and perform transaction. However, the limitation of the work is that, whenever the user initiate the service firstly he/she enters the username and the user redirected to another screen which prompted to enter the One Time Password that has been delivered on to the users registered mobile number at that particular moment of time. There are drawbacks to this approach. First, it pushes extra costs onto some end users, particularly in North America, where customers must pay for the messages they receive. Second, it is subject to network coverage, network latency and SMS delivery issues, which creates uncertainty over whether SMSs will be delivered quickly, or at all. Third, it doesn't address the Man-in-the-Middle fraud problem.

CHAPTER 3

SYSTEM ANALYSIS AND DESIGN

3.1 INTRODUCTION

This chapter reviews and evaluates the performance of the existing platform with a direction of designing the newly proposed platform. It discusses the processes used in carrying out the study and also provides an outline of research design and the instruments for data collection.

3.2 THE EXISTING SYSTEM

The existing mobile banking card less transaction platform by wema bank alat application is characterized by security flaws. The Alat application by wema like other mobile banking application is a banking application that is yet to embrace the full potentials that information technology provides. When a user logs into the mobile application to perform cashless transaction a pay-code is generated this is then sent to the user mobile phone. This method is highly insecure as theft of mobile phone during the process, cloning of the registered sim card can lead to theft and ATM fraud.

3.3 THE PROPOSED SYSTEM

Due to limitations and problems of the existing platform, a new platform to solve the impending internet banking security problems of the existing platform stated above is being proposed. The new platform which will retain the existing name (Alat by Wema) is expected on implementation to fulfil the following requirements;

   a) Authenticate user before allowing transactions.
   b) During cashless transactions, users will get their pay-code request embedded in a digital image.
   c) A database of records which will save all digital images sent by the users to the server for embedding of pay-code.
   d) Facilitates good and secure services delivery to it users.
   e) Provides a better secure platform for users to carry out it transactions.

3.3.1 ELEMENTS OF THE PROPOSED SYSTEM

The proposed platform will have the following elements:

User Interface: it is an interactive page that enables the user to navigate through the different pages that makes up the platform.

Portals: A portal provides a starting point or gateway to other resources on the internet or intranet.

Database: This act as the store house where data most especially the digital images are stored.

3.4 DESIGN TOOLS

JAVA

Java is a programming language that produces software for multiple platforms. When a programmer writes a Java application, the compiled code (known as bytecode) runs on most operating systems (OS), including Windows, Linux and Mac OS. Java derives much of its syntax from the C and C++ programming languages. (www.techopedia.com)

NETBEANS

NetBeans is an integrated development environment (IDE) for Java. NetBeans allows applications to be developed from a set of modular software components called modules. NetBeans runs on Microsoft Windows, macOS, Linux and Solaris. In addition to Java development, it has extensions for other languages like PHP, C, C++, HTML5 , and JavaScript Applications based on NetBeans, including the NetBeans IDE, can be extended by third party developers.

ANDROID STUDIO

Android Studio is the Integrated Development Environment (IDE) for Android that was developed by google as an alternate to the previously used Eclipse. Android Studio is based on Java IDE called Intelli. Android Studio comes bundled with its own version of the Android SDK, which is preconfigured to be used with Android studio upon installation. Android Studio IDE is comprised of a vast array of panels, tools, and functions to aid productivity when developing android applications.

FIREBASE

Firebase is a real-time database that power's application backend developed by google, including data storage, user authentication, static hosting, and more. It focus on creating extraordinary user experiences. It offers simple control dashboard and since it is real-time, every change made will automatically update connected clients.

3.5 DESIGN OF THE PROPOSED SYSTEM

The platform design breaks down the system into modules and steps. Its aim is to create a structure that will implement the functions expressed in the platform specification. This design will express the development of a conceptual view of the system; identifying the processing functions and the working functions. There are portals in this platform through which the users interact with the system.

After the user might have passed through the normal authentication process on the mobile application, the user is presented with the two menus above when he wants to request or get his pay-code.

The request code menu provides the user with an interface to request for the amount he wants to withdraw and to upload an image he wants the code to be embedded in at the server side. It provides a link to the user's gallery to choose a picture of his choice that will be used as digital image for the embedding of the pay-code.

The get-code menu provides the user an avenue to decode the embedded image after the user might have downloaded it back from the mail or as a multimedia message from his mobile phone. When the get-code menu is clicked, the user is presented with an interface that requires to choose the image he downloaded to the phone gallery in order to decode and display the pay-code for the card less transaction.

3.6 SYSTEM USE CASE DIAGRAM

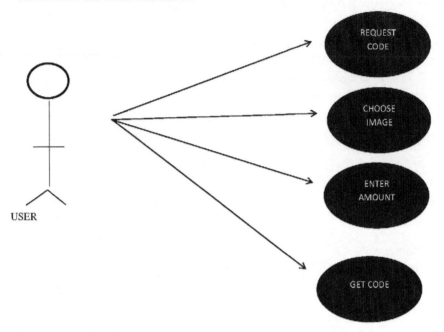

Figure 3.1 System Use Case Diagram

3.7 SYSTEM ARCHITECTURE

The system works like this: the cardless withdrawal system will be integrated into the Alat mobile banking application and will be available to the user from the menu bar.

When making a cardless cash transaction request, few steps will be required of the user to take. First, the user will select the account from which he wants money to be withdrawn. Next, the user will select the request code option from where the user will be taken to a portal where he will have to upload from his gallery an image he wants his code to be embedded in at the bank server side. After selecting image the user will be prompt to enter the amount of money he wants to withdraw from his account so that the encoding can start at the server side as soon as possible. After the request has been sent, it will be processed by the banking server. If the user has the requested amount in his account and hasn't exceeded the daily limit, the transaction will be approved and a random, unique 6 digit transaction code known as (pay-code) will be generated

29

on the server. This code will be embedded in the image previously uploaded to the bank server by the user and will be sent through SMS or Email to the smartphone of the user to be downloaded as multimedia message. In order to ensure a higher level of security, the pay-code will expire if not used in the next fifteen minutes after it has been generated.

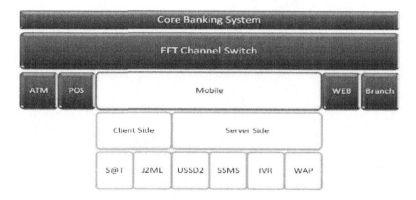

Figure3.2 Mobile banking Architecture in overall banking architecture. (Source, Financialquest.com)

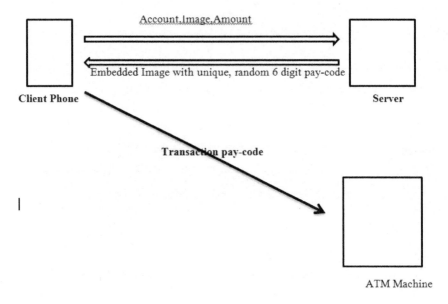

Figure 3.3 Architecture of the proposed platform.

3.8 THE CARD LESS STEGANOGRAPHY SYSTEM

A secured card less steganography platform can be realized using LSB and Firebase which provides a real-time database and backend as a service.

3.8.1 FIREBASE CLOUD DATABASE

The service provides an API that allows application data to be synchronized across clients and stored on **Firebase's** cloud. Firebase Store and sync data with NoSQL cloud **database**. The data is then synced across all clients in real-time, and remains available when the mobile app goes offline. The **Firebase** Real-time **Database** is a cloud-hosted **database**. Data is stored as JSON and synchronized in real-time to every connected client.

3.8.2 LSB ENCODING

Least significance bit (LSB)-based steganography is one of the simplest techniques that hide a secret message in the LSBs of pixel values by introducing imperceptible distortions. It is a spatial domain method.

STEPS INVOLVED IN LSB ENCODING AND DECODING

a. Steps for embedding the pay-code in the digital image:

1. Image to be used as cover image was read and little noise was added to make it easier to disguise changes due to embedding the message image.

2. Image to be sued as message image was read.

3. Bit planes of each image were separated.

4. The least 4 bitplanes of cover image was replaced with the 4 most significant bitplanes from message image.

5. The resultant Steganographic image was retrieved by recombining these bitplanes.

b. Retrieving message image:

1. The steganographic image was read.

2. The required number of bitplanes from the image was extracted

3. The lower four bitplanes were recombined and it gave the retrieved message image.

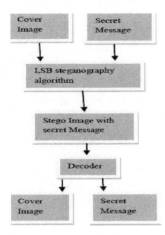

Figure 3.4 LSB Image Steganography Process

CHAPTER FOUR

SYSTEM IMPLEMENTATION AND TESTING

4.1 INTRODUCTION

This chapter deals with how the system is developed and implemented. The system development could be seen as the simple process of writing programs to solve the needs of the user. The system implementation consists of the preparation of the resources including equipment and personnel with the testing of the system.

It describes the implementation of the card less steganography platform.

4.1.1 SYSTEM REQUIREMENTS

The system requirements for the card less steganography platform are shown in the table below:

Table 4.1: System requirements

S/N	Hardware Requirements	Software Requirements
1.	1Gb Ram, 2Gb Ram	5.0 Android version
2.	4Gb internal memory (ROM)	

4.2 **Homepage**: This is the index of the page where a user is provided with options to choose from depending on the user's action. The homepage is shown in the figure below

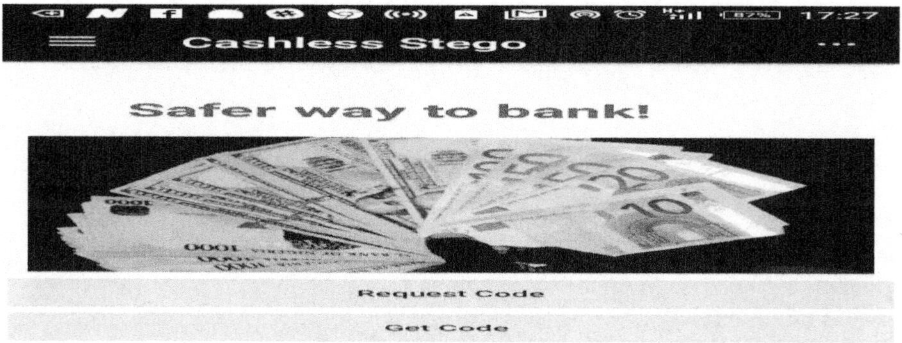

Figure 4.1: Homepage

From the homepage above, the request code link is mainly for users to make request for the pay-code in order to carry out their card less transaction. The request code link when clicked will open the page shown in figure 4.2 below. The page opens with various options for the user to make a choice depending on what he/she wants at that particular time.

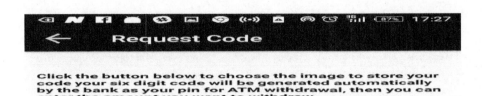

Figure 4.2 **Request Code Link**

Here, the users choose from the gallery images they wants the code to be embedded into. It is the image they chose here that will be sent to the server for encryption of the pay-code into the image.

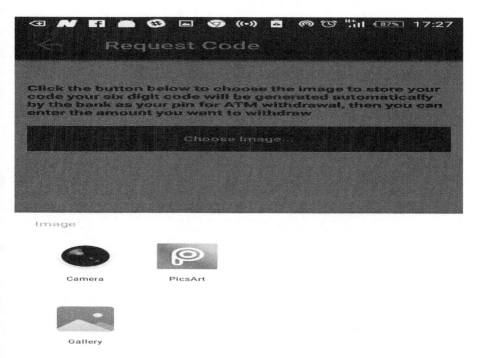

Figure 4.3 Select Image Interface

Figure 4.3 above is where the user will select the image that will be uploaded to the server. The user might decide to choose from gallery or snap a new picture with the smartphone camera.

Figure 4.4 Enter amount to be withdrawn portal.

Figure 4.4 above is where the user will enter the amount he wants to withdraw from his bank account after he might have uploaded his preferred image to the bank server.

Click the button below to choose the image to store your code your six digit code will be generated automatically by the bank as your pin for ATM withdrawal, then you can enter the amount you want to withdraw

Get Code

Figure 4.5 Get Code button

This is where the user will get his code to make the cardless withdrawal, this happens after he might have downloaded the multimedia message via SMS or Email.

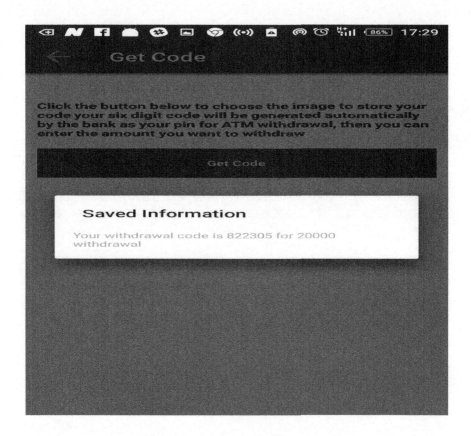

Figure 4.6 the interface of the pay-code for the cardless transaction

Figure 4.6 above opens when the user decodes the image he downloaded as multimedia message.

CHAPTER 5

CONCLUSION AND RECOMMENDATION

5.1 CONCLUSION

The importance of Mobile banking can never be overemphasizing, no bank service is convenient, effective and efficient as mobile banking. Mobile banking offers its customers with a wide range of services, customers are able to interact and make transactions with their bank accounts from anywhere in the world without time restrictions. In order for this to continue to grow, the security and privacy aspects have to be improved. The security model used for mobile banking by most banks is strongly based on mobile banking user identification and authentication methods, which are also components where most mobile banking systems' vulnerabilities are found.

This project discuss extensively current problems arising in the mobile banking services been offered, the need to better secure mobile banking using image steganography as the future of electronic banking will be a system where users are able to interact with their banks "worry-free" without fear of compromising their rights and interests. However, manipulation of the image such as cropping or resizing of the downloaded image from server can make the information embedded in the digital image gets missing.

5.2 RECOMMENDATION

Mobile banking is not a static concept but one that is constantly changing and as it is changing, the security measures should also change to keep up the standard. As a result of conclusion gotten from this project work, I recommend that the system developed and implemented should be deployed to serve the purpose to which it was designed and developed. The system provides a platform for further improvements. For secured mobile banking to be a reality, customers' confidential information should be well protected by the banks and should not be misused.

REFERENCES

Barskar, Deen, Ahemed and Bharti, "The Algorithm Analysis of E-commerce Security Issues for Online Payment Transaction System in Banking Technology" IJCSIS, Vol.8, no.1, April 2010.

Bhosale, (2012) Security in E-Banking via Card less Biometric ATMs

Billa, 'Security Issues in Mobile Banking''.

DivyaVermaGakhar "Security Issues in E-Banking", PIMT Journal of Research, Vol.1, No.1, March-August 2008, pp. 29-34

GunajitSarma and Pranavsingh "Internet Banking: Risk Analysis and Applicability of Biometric Technology for authentication" International Journal Pure Application Science Technology" (2010), pp. 67-78, ISSN 2229-6107, www.ijopaasat.in

Innocent and Adewale. (2016). Securing Card less Automated Teller Machine Transactions Using Bimodal Authentication System.

Krishnaveni and Sathyadevi, (2017) Mobile Banking and its Security

Lichtenstein & Williamson: Consumer Adoption of Internet Banking, Journal of Electronic Commerce, Research VOL 7, No.2, 2006

Manoharan, B. 2007, "Indian E-payment System and its Performance", Professional Banker, Vol.7, No.3, pp.61-69.

Neenu and Harsh (2014). Card less Cash Access Using Biometric ATM Security System.

Omariba, Masese and Wanyebi, (2012) Security and Privacy of Electronic Banking.

Prerana and Nikumbh. (2015). Security System in ATM using Multimodal Biometric System and Steganographic Technique.

Rao, GurleenKour and DivyaJyoti, (2011) One Time Password Security through Cryptography for Mobile Banking

Sarhan, Ahmed and Safwant, (2015) Secured Android Based Mobile Banking Scheme.

41

Shazmeen and shyam, (2012) A Practical Approach for Secure Internet Banking based on
Cryptography

SyedaFarhaShazmeen, Shyam Prasad, A Practical Approach for secure Internet Banking Based
on Cryptography, International Journal of Scientific and Research Publication, vol 2, Issue 12,
Dec 2012, ISSN 2250-3153, www.ijsrp.org

Wendy W.N. Wan "Customers" adoption of banking channels in Hong Kong" International
Journal of BankMarketing 04/2005; 23(3):255-272

Zachary, Nelson and Dr. Wanyembi, "Security and Privacy of Electronic Banking" IJCSI, Vol.
9, Issue 4 No. 3, July 2012, ISSN: 1694-0814

Printed in Great Britain
by Amazon

10484766R00037